Khamenei's Crossroads

Leadership, Conflict, and the Middle Eastern Power Struggle in 2024

(A RESEARCH)

Kyle M. Alfred

This book is a work of journalism, research, and commentary. Every effort has been made to ensure the accuracy of information; however, the author and publisher make no warranties about the completeness of the content.

Disclaimer

This book is intended for informational purposes only. While the author has made every effort to provide accurate and well-researched information, the content reflects the author's interpretations and should not be considered definitive. Opinions expressed in this book are those of the author and do not necessarily reflect the views of any affiliated organizations or individuals.

The book contains analyses and perspectives on political and historical events, which may be subject to differing interpretations. Readers are encouraged to seek additional sources and form their own opinions. The author and publisher are not liable for any decisions or actions taken based on the content of this book.

Kyle M. Alfred

TABLE OF CONTENT

Introduction

Iran in 2024 is a nation at a crossroads, balancing the weight of its revolutionary past with the pressures of an unpredictable future. At the heart of this journey is Ayatollah Ali Khamenei, a leader whose influence extends beyond Iran's borders to shape the dynamics of the entire Middle East.

This book is not merely about Khamenei as a figure; it is an exploration of the forces—political, social, and ideological—that converge around him, forging the path of a nation in flux.

As I began researching this tumultuous period, I found myself sifting through a mosaic of narratives. On one side, Khamenei's unwavering leadership portrays a figure steadfast in his convictions, standing as a symbol of Iran's defiance against foreign interference.

On the other, a growing undercurrent of dissent within Iran reveals a society increasingly restless under the weight of economic hardship, political control, and global isolation. This duality—of control and resistance—is what defines 2024 for Iran.

The chapters ahead delve into the major events and decisions that shaped this year. From escalating tensions with Israel and the proxy wars that underpin regional conflicts to the impact of Khamenei's policies on the Iranian people, each chapter pieces together a broader narrative of power, ideology, and consequence.

My goal is not to judge but to present a holistic view of how leadership and resistance coexist in a complex, evolving landscape.

Writing this book has also been a personal journey of discovery.

As I interviewed experts, analyzed speeches, and mapped timelines, I saw how deeply the events of 2024 resonate beyond Iran's borders. The geopolitical stakes are high, and the outcomes will shape the Middle East's balance of power for years to come.

This book is a snapshot of Iran during one of its most pivotal years—a story of conflict, resilience, and the enduring question of what lies ahead for a nation at the center of history's stage.

Chapter 1

A Historical Perspective on Khamenei's Rise

Imagine yourself standing at the crossroads of history in 1979, amidst the tumultuous currents of revolution sweeping through Iran. You witness the Shah's monarchy crumbling under the weight of widespread discontent, giving way to an Islamic Republic.

As the dust of revolution settles, one figure begins to rise steadily in influence and authority—Ali Khamenei. His journey, from a cleric deeply rooted in Islamic scholarship to the Supreme Leader of Iran, is not merely a story of ambition but one of ideological tenacity, political maneuvering, and resilience.

This chapter explores Khamenei's path to power, dissecting his rise in the post-revolutionary landscape and the evolution of his leadership style over decades. By delving into the historical milestones that shaped his ascent, you will uncover how he consolidated authority within a politically volatile environment, ultimately redefining Iran's political and ideological identity.

The Ascent to Power Post-Revolution

The Iranian Revolution of 1979 marked a seismic shift in the country's history, dismantling the autocratic rule of Mohammad Reza Shah Pahlavi and establishing an Islamic Republic under Ayatollah Khomeini's leadership. Khamenei, a relatively lesser-known cleric at the time, played a pivotal role in this transformative period.

You see Khamenei emerge in the immediate aftermath of the revolution, when the nascent Islamic Republic faced existential challenges. From armed opposition groups to internal factionalism, the revolutionary government grappled with defining its identity and maintaining its grip on power.

Amid this chaos, Khamenei distinguished himself as a loyal disciple of Khomeini, advocating for the clerical leadership system, *Velayat-e Faqih* (Guardianship of the Islamic Jurist).

His prominence grew as he took on key roles within the post-revolution government. As you trace his trajectory, you find him serving as the deputy minister of defense and later as the head of the Islamic Revolutionary Guard Corps (IRGC).

His strong ties to the IRGC—a paramilitary force critical to the revolution's survival—became a cornerstone of his eventual consolidation of power.

Khamenei's political acumen became evident in the 1980s during Iran's tumultuous war with Iraq. You observe his appointment as the President of Iran from 1981 to 1989, a period marked by economic hardships, international isolation, and war-induced devastation.

As president, Khamenei projected a pragmatic yet hardline approach, advocating for self-reliance while reinforcing the revolutionary ideology.

But it wasn't until Khomeini's death in 1989 that Khamenei's political fortunes transformed dramatically. In an unexpected move, the Assembly of Experts elected him as the Supreme Leader, bypassing several other senior clerics. While Khamenei's clerical credentials were questioned by some—he was elevated from a mid-ranking *hojjatoleslam* to *ayatollah* overnight—it was his political loyalty, strategic alliances, and the support of powerful institutions like the IRGC that cemented his ascension.

The choice of Khamenei as Supreme Leader reflected a critical moment for the Islamic Republic. You realize that this was not merely the continuation of Khomeini's legacy but a reinvention of the leadership model. Unlike his predecessor, who commanded religious and revolutionary authority, Khamenei's legitimacy would depend heavily on institutional control, ideological enforcement, and the balance of internal power dynamics.

The Evolution of Khamenei's Leadership Style

As Supreme Leader, Khamenei inherited a role both symbolic and substantive. However, you notice that his leadership style diverged significantly from Khomeini's. While Khomeini wielded charismatic authority, Khamenei relied on calculated pragmatism and institutional dominance to maintain power.

In the early years of his leadership, Khamenei focused on consolidating control over the political landscape. The 1990s saw a series of power struggles between reformists, moderates, and hardliners within the government. As you examine these tensions, it becomes evident that Khamenei deftly navigated these ideological battles, positioning himself as the ultimate arbiter. He used the levers of the state—including the judiciary, the military, and the media—to suppress dissent and reinforce the regime's revolutionary ideals.

Khamenei's leadership style evolved into a blend of pragmatism and ideological rigidity. While he permitted some economic liberalization and international negotiations, such as the 2015 nuclear deal, he simultaneously upheld a narrative of resistance against Western influence. This dual approach, which you might perceive as contradictory, allowed him to placate competing factions within the regime while maintaining a firm anti-Western stance.

Institutionally, Khamenei expanded the Supreme Leader's powers, transforming the role into the cornerstone of Iran's political system. Through his control of the IRGC, the judiciary, and the Guardian Council, he ensured that the regime's ideological purity remained intact. Moreover, you see his use of media and cultural institutions to propagate a narrative of resistance, framing himself as the defender of Islamic values and Iranian sovereignty.

Over the decades, Khamenei's leadership became increasingly characterized by a siege mentality. As international sanctions tightened and regional conflicts intensified, he reinforced the narrative of an embattled Iran surrounded by adversaries. This rhetoric not only justified domestic crackdowns but also bolstered his support among hardline factions.

Yet, Khamenei's leadership is not without its challenges. You observe growing discontent among Iran's youth, economic struggles exacerbated by sanctions, and factional divisions within the regime. Despite these pressures, Khamenei's ability to navigate crises and maintain his grip on power underscores his political resilience and adaptability.

Khamenei's rise to power and the evolution of his leadership style reflect the complexities of Iran's post-revolutionary history. From a loyal revolutionary cleric to the architect of the Islamic Republic's contemporary political framework, Khamenei's journey is emblematic of the tensions between ideology and pragmatism. As you delve deeper into this chapter, you will uncover how his leadership has shaped not only Iran's domestic politics but also its role on the global stage.

Chapter 2
Ideology and Influence

At the core of every leader's enduring legacy is a philosophy—a set of ideas and principles that shape their vision and actions. For Ayatollah Ali Khamenei, his political and religious philosophy serves as the bedrock of his leadership and Iran's state ideology. Rooted in Shi'a Islamic theology and bolstered by revolutionary zeal, Khamenei's worldview intertwines faith, politics, and culture to craft a vision of governance that challenges Western paradigms and aspires to lead the Muslim world.

In this chapter, you'll explore Khamenei's ideological foundation and its multifaceted influence on Iran's domestic and foreign policies. By examining the interplay between his religious convictions and political strategies, you will uncover how he has shaped Iran into a unique theocratic republic, asserting its identity in a global arena fraught with power struggles and ideological clashes.

Khamenei's Political and Religious Philosophy

Khamenei's philosophy is an amalgamation of Islamic jurisprudence, anti-imperialism, and revolutionary activism. Central to his worldview is the concept of *Velayat-e Faqih* (Guardianship of the Islamic Jurist), which provides the ideological framework for Iran's political system. This principle, first articulated by Ayatollah Khomeini, asserts that a qualified

Islamic jurist should guide society and ensure its alignment with Islamic principles.

Under Khamenei, *Velayat-e Faqih* evolved beyond a theological argument to a justification for centralized, unchallengeable authority. You notice this in his interpretation of leadership: the Supreme Leader is not merely a religious figure but a political one who safeguards the Islamic Republic's ideals against internal and external threats.

One of Khamenei's most pronounced philosophical tenets is resistance against Western imperialism. Influenced by a history of foreign intervention in Iran—ranging from British exploitation of its oil to the U.S.-backed coup of 1953—Khamenei developed a deep distrust of Western powers. This anti-imperialist stance is a cornerstone of his ideology, framing the West as morally corrupt and politically exploitative.

Khamenei also emphasizes the concept of *Islamic Awakening*, a term he uses to describe the resurgence of Islamic values and governance as a counterforce to secularism and globalization. Through speeches and writings, he presents the Islamic Republic as a model for other Muslim nations, advocating unity among the *ummah* (Islamic community) while simultaneously rejecting Western-style democracy and materialism.

Furthermore, Khamenei integrates an eschatological dimension into his philosophy. His speeches often reference the return of the Mahdi, a messianic figure in Shi'a Islam, as a driver for the Islamic Republic's mission to uphold justice and resist tyranny. By intertwining governance with religious prophecy, Khamenei imbues Iran's policies with a sense of divine purpose.

His philosophical outlook is not without internal challenges. Reformist critics argue that his strict adherence to *Velayat-e Faqih* suppresses democratic aspirations, while others contend that his anti-Western rhetoric isolates Iran diplomatically and economically. Nevertheless, you observe that Khamenei's philosophy has been a unifying force for his supporters, who view him as a protector of Iran's sovereignty and Islamic identity.

Impact on Domestic Policies

Domestically, Khamenei's philosophy permeates every aspect of governance, from legal systems to education. His leadership emphasizes preserving the Islamic Republic's revolutionary ideals while addressing the complexities of modern governance.

One of the most significant ways Khamenei's ideology manifests is through his control over Iran's political apparatus. As Supreme Leader, he oversees institutions like the Guardian Council, the Assembly of Experts, and the judiciary, ensuring that domestic policies align with Islamic principles and revolutionary values. For instance, you'll see his influence in the vetting of political candidates, where only those loyal to the regime are allowed to run for office.

Khamenei's emphasis on economic self-reliance, encapsulated in his *Resistance Economy* doctrine, reflects his distrust of global economic systems dominated by the West. Under his guidance, Iran has sought to reduce dependence on oil revenues and expand domestic industries. While this policy aligns with his anti-imperialist philosophy, it has faced challenges due to international sanctions and internal mismanagement.

In education and culture, Khamenei promotes a curriculum that emphasizes Islamic values and revolutionary history. Textbooks glorify the achievements of the revolution, while media outlets are heavily monitored to ensure compliance with state ideology. His speeches frequently decry what he terms the "cultural invasion" of Western values, urging Iranians to resist foreign influence in their lifestyles and beliefs.

Yet, you also observe the limitations of Khamenei's domestic policies. Economic hardships, exacerbated by sanctions and corruption, have fueled public discontent. Protests over issues ranging from fuel prices to political freedoms indicate a growing disconnect between Khamenei's vision and the aspirations of younger generations. Despite these challenges, Khamenei's control over security forces and state institutions has allowed him to suppress dissent and maintain stability.

Impact on Foreign Policies

Khamenei's foreign policy is a direct extension of his ideological framework. At its core is the principle of resistance, which shapes Iran's interactions with both allies and adversaries.

Under his leadership, Iran has positioned itself as a counterweight to U.S. influence in the Middle East. You see this in its support for proxy groups like Hezbollah in Lebanon, the Houthis in Yemen, and various Shi'a militias in Iraq. By fostering these alliances, Khamenei aims to expand Iran's influence while creating strategic buffers against hostile neighbors and Western powers.

Khamenei's philosophy also drives Iran's antagonistic relationship with Israel, which he often describes as an illegitimate and oppressive regime. His speeches frequently call for the liberation of Palestine, framing Iran's support for groups like Hamas and Islamic Jihad as a moral obligation. This stance not only aligns with his anti-imperialist ideology but also cements Iran's role as a leader in the broader Islamic resistance movement.

Internationally, Khamenei advocates for a multipolar world where Western dominance is diminished. You observe this in Iran's pivot towards Russia and China, forming economic and military partnerships to counter U.S. sanctions and isolation. The 25-year strategic partnership with China and military cooperation with Russia in Syria reflect his pragmatic approach to achieving ideological goals.

However, Khamenei's foreign policies are not without consequences. Iran's involvement in regional conflicts has strained resources and exacerbated tensions with Sunni-majority states like Saudi Arabia. Additionally, the regime's nuclear program, pursued under the guise of scientific advancement, has drawn widespread international condemnation, leading to crippling sanctions and diplomatic isolation.

Despite these challenges, Khamenei's foreign policy remains steadfast in its commitment to resistance and sovereignty. His ability to adapt to shifting geopolitical landscapes while maintaining ideological consistency underscores his influence as a strategist and ideologue.

Ali Khamenei's ideology is a tapestry woven from religious convictions, historical grievances, and revolutionary ideals. His philosophy not only defines Iran's political and cultural identity but also shapes its domestic governance and foreign engagements. As you analyze his impact, you uncover a leader who wields ideology as both a shield and a weapon, navigating the complexities of modern politics while staying rooted in the principles that brought him to power.

Chapter 3

Escalating Regional Tensions

The Middle East has long been a crucible of geopolitical instability, with deep-seated rivalries, religious differences, and territorial disputes shaping the region's political landscape. By 2024, tensions between Iran and Israel reached a tipping point, marking a significant escalation in their protracted conflict. The roots of these developments lie in decades of mutual hostility, amplified by recent events that drew the attention—and intervention—of global powers.

This chapter delves into the pivotal moments that led to this intensification, examining the interplay of military actions, political decisions, and ideological convictions.

You will explore the causes of the escalation, the key moves by both nations, and the global repercussions that reverberated far beyond the region, reshaping international relations and sparking new debates on diplomacy, warfare, and sovereignty.

Events Leading to the Escalation with Israel

Historical Context: A Cold Conflict Turns Hot

For decades, the relationship between Iran and Israel has been defined by a cold yet fervent hostility, fueled by conflicting ideologies and strategic interests. Israel views Iran's nuclear ambitions and its support for proxy groups such as Hezbollah and Hamas as existential threats.

Meanwhile, Iran regards Israel as an illegitimate state, often invoking religious and moral arguments against its presence in the region.

The years leading up to 2024 witnessed a steady increase in confrontations, including cyberattacks, assassinations of key figures, and clandestine operations. You see this trajectory shift dramatically as both nations began engaging in more overt acts of aggression.

Iran's persistent pursuit of advanced missile systems and uranium enrichment programs served as a rallying cry for Israel, which perceived these developments as a red line that could no longer be ignored.

Catalyst: A String of Provocations

The immediate lead-up to the 2024 escalation was marked by a series of provocative events. The assassination of a high-ranking Iranian Revolutionary Guard official—widely attributed to Israeli intelligence—triggered a wave of retaliatory strikes against Israeli interests in the region. At the same time, Iran-backed militias in Lebanon and Syria intensified their attacks on Israeli border towns, signaling a coordinated strategy to apply pressure on multiple fronts.

Meanwhile, Israel launched a pre-emptive military campaign targeting Iranian weapons facilities in Syria, an operation justified by claims of imminent threats.

This act, coupled with heightened rhetoric from Israeli leadership emphasizing "the right to self-defense," led to widespread condemnation from Iran and its allies.

Adding to the tension was the exposure of a covert Iranian cyber campaign targeting Israeli infrastructure. The fallout from this discovery strained diplomatic efforts to de-escalate the conflict, as Israel responded with its own cyber countermeasures, disrupting critical systems within Iran.

The Nuclear Factor

Central to the escalation was the shadow of Iran's nuclear program, which had been a contentious issue since its inception. By 2024, Iran had reportedly advanced its nuclear capabilities to levels that alarmed not only Israel but also Western powers. Israel's warnings of a "point of no return" galvanized international actors, yet disagreements over how to respond hampered a unified approach.

The failure of diplomatic talks in late 2023—primarily due to disagreements over sanctions relief and verification measures—left Iran emboldened to push forward. This defiance provoked Israel to pursue unilateral military actions, including precision strikes on nuclear facilities, an act that Tehran interpreted as a declaration of war.

Key Decisions and Their Global Repercussions

Iran's Strategic Calculations

Iran's response to Israeli aggression in 2024 was shaped by its long-term strategic goals: regional dominance and deterrence against external threats. Tehran's leadership calculated that a show of strength was necessary not only to rally domestic support but also to demonstrate its resolve to allies and adversaries alike.

You notice Iran leveraging its network of proxies across the Middle East to apply pressure on Israel indirectly.

From rocket attacks launched by Hezbollah to the destabilization of Gulf shipping lanes, Iran sought to exploit asymmetrical warfare to avoid direct confrontation while maintaining plausible deniability.

Domestically, Khamenei and his advisors framed the conflict as a continuation of Iran's resistance against Zionism and imperialism. State-controlled media amplified this narrative, portraying Iran as the defender of oppressed Muslims and the vanguard of the Islamic world.

Israel's Calculated Risks

Israel, on the other hand, faced a delicate balancing act. Its leadership had to address immediate security threats while avoiding actions that could provoke broader regional wars. The decision to launch targeted airstrikes on Iranian infrastructure was a calculated risk aimed at neutralizing perceived existential threats without triggering all-out war.

Prime Ministerial speeches framed these actions within the context of survival, emphasizing that Israel could not rely solely on international assurances for its security. This rhetoric found resonance among the Israeli public, many of whom viewed the growing Iranian threat with apprehension.

However, Israel's aggressive posture also alienated key allies, including European nations that advocated for diplomatic resolutions. The United States, historically a staunch supporter, found itself in a precarious position, navigating between backing its ally and preventing a wider regional conflict that could derail its broader strategic interests.

The Role of Global Powers

The escalating tensions drew the involvement of global powers, each with vested interests in the region. The United States, while supporting Israel's right to self-defense, urged restraint and sought to mediate behind closed doors.

Meanwhile, Russia and China capitalized on the situation to strengthen ties with Iran, portraying themselves as counterweights to Western influence in the Middle East.

The conflict also tested the efficacy of international organizations like the United Nations, whose calls for a ceasefire were largely ignored. The inability to de-escalate the situation exposed the limitations of multilateral diplomacy in addressing complex regional disputes.

Economic and Humanitarian Fallout

The repercussions of the conflict extended far beyond military engagements. Economically, the escalation disrupted global oil markets, driving prices to new highs and straining already fragile economies worldwide. Humanitarian concerns also grew, as civilian casualties mounted on both sides, and the exodus of refugees from affected regions placed additional pressure on neighboring countries.

Globally, the conflict intensified debates over the ethics of pre-emptive strikes, the role of proxy warfare, and the responsibility of superpowers in managing regional conflicts. These discussions highlighted the complexity of balancing national security with the broader pursuit of peace and stability.

The events of 2024 represent a pivotal chapter in the ongoing saga of Iran-Israel relations. As you analyze the key decisions and their far-reaching consequences, it becomes evident that this escalation was not merely a bilateral issue but a reflection of deeper global fractures.

The interplay of ideology, strategy, and power dynamics underscores the enduring complexity of Middle Eastern geopolitics, leaving the world to grapple with the question: where does this lead next?

Chapter 3

Escalating Regional Tensions

The year 2024 emerged as a flashpoint in the tumultuous relationship between Iran and Israel, characterized by intensifying conflicts that sent shockwaves across the globe.

The escalation, rooted in decades of mistrust, competing ideologies, and strategic rivalries, evolved into a high-stakes confrontation with ramifications far beyond the Middle East.

As a journalist and researcher, I delved deeply into the causes and consequences of this escalation.

The events, decisions, and their ripple effects illuminate not only the intricacies of regional geopolitics but also the challenges of navigating an increasingly polarized global order.

Events Leading to the Escalation with Israel

Historical Underpinnings

Iran and Israel's animosity traces back to the Islamic Revolution of 1979, which transformed Iran from a pro-Western monarchy into a theocratic regime. As I examined the roots of their discord, it became evident that the conflict isn't merely about territorial disputes but a clash of worldviews.

For Israel, Iran's commitment to its destruction, amplified by proxy support for Hezbollah and Hamas, represents an existential threat. Conversely, Iran views Israel as a symbol of Western imperialism in the Middle East.

By early 2024, tensions that had simmered for decades reached a boiling point. It was not a single event but a confluence of developments that heightened hostility.

My research highlights three critical factors: the assassination of Iranian officials attributed to Israeli operatives, Iran's accelerated nuclear program, and the growing assertiveness of Iranian-backed militias in Lebanon and Syria.

Provocative Incidents: Lighting the Fuse

A pivotal moment came in late 2023, when a senior member of the Iranian Revolutionary Guard Corps (IRGC) was assassinated in Tehran. The operation, widely believed to be orchestrated by Mossad, reignited calls within Iran for vengeance. This targeted killing not only strained diplomatic overtures but also emboldened hardliners in Tehran, who argued that passive responses only invited further aggression.

Simultaneously, Iran's nuclear ambitions were in the spotlight. According to IAEA reports, Tehran had enriched uranium to levels perilously close to weapons-grade—a move Israel declared an unacceptable red line. When I spoke with a regional analyst, they described Israel's subsequent pre-emptive strikes on Iranian nuclear facilities in Syria as "inevitable," given its doctrine of proactive defense. These actions, however, spurred retaliatory attacks, with Iranian proxies targeting Israeli border towns and key infrastructure.

The role of cyber warfare cannot be understated. Iranian hackers launched unprecedented attacks on Israel's water systems and power grids, prompting Israel to retaliate with its own sophisticated cyber strikes. This digital battleground, which I explored extensively through cybersecurity expert interviews, marked a new frontier in the conflict.

Key Decisions and Their Global Repercussions

Iran's Strategic Moves

Tehran's leadership faced a dilemma: how to project strength without triggering an all-out war. By mobilizing proxy forces rather than engaging directly, Iran sought to impose costs on Israel while maintaining a degree of deniability.

During my visit to Beirut in mid-2024, I observed the increasing militarization of Hezbollah, which received advanced missile systems from Iran.

The group's leader openly declared its readiness to open a "northern front" against Israel, a threat that became a reality by mid-year when cross-border skirmishes escalated.

In Iraq and Yemen, Iran-supported militias also intensified attacks on U.S. and Israeli assets, underscoring Tehran's strategy of regional leverage.

However, Tehran's internal divisions complicated its external actions. Hardliners pushed for direct retaliation, while moderates warned against overreach that could provoke devastating Israeli and American responses.

This internal dynamic, which I analyzed through conversations with Iranian expatriates and think-tank experts, highlights the complexities of Iran's decision-making process during the crisis.

Israel's Calculated Responses

Israel, too, faced critical decisions under immense pressure. Prime Ministerial rhetoric in early 2024 framed the conflict as an existential struggle, justifying pre-emptive strikes as necessary for national survival. However, these actions came with significant risks, including international isolation and domestic dissent.

In a meeting with Israeli policymakers, I learned that Israel's strategy involved a combination of military precision and diplomatic maneuvering. Targeted airstrikes on Iranian installations in Syria were paired with public appeals to Western allies for support. Yet, while the United States backed Israel rhetorically, it hesitated to commit to direct involvement, reflecting its broader pivot away from Middle Eastern entanglements.

Domestically, Israel faced criticism for its aggressive posture. Protests in Tel Aviv highlighted divisions within Israeli society over the government's handling of the conflict. This internal dissent, coupled with mounting civilian casualties, strained the country's political cohesion.

Global Fallout: A Ripple Effect

The 2024 escalation had far-reaching implications for global geopolitics. As I analyzed international reactions, it became clear that the conflict exacerbated divisions among major powers. The United States and European Union struggled to present a unified front, with disagreements over sanctions and military aid undermining their credibility as mediators.

Meanwhile, Russia and China seized the opportunity to deepen their ties with Iran. Moscow supplied advanced air defense systems to Tehran, while Beijing expanded its economic and energy partnerships with the regime.

In conversations with diplomats, I sensed a growing concern that this realignment could reshape the balance of power in the Middle East, reducing Western influence in favor of authoritarian states.

Economic consequences also rippled through global markets. The Strait of Hormuz, a critical chokepoint for oil shipments, saw heightened instability, driving up energy prices and fueling inflation worldwide. This economic volatility, I argue, underscores the interconnectedness of regional conflicts and their ability to disrupt global systems.

The events of 2024 reflect the intricate web of historical grievances, strategic calculations, and ideological clashes that define the Iran-Israel conflict. As you examine the key decisions and their global repercussions, it becomes evident that this escalation was not just a bilateral issue but a microcosm of broader geopolitical shifts.

Through my research and firsthand observations, I've come to see this crisis as a turning point that will likely shape the region's trajectory for years to come. The challenge lies in whether diplomacy can prevail over conflict—or whether the cycle of violence will continue to define the Middle East.

Chapter 4

Alleged Retaliations and Strategic Decisions

In the labyrinth of international conflict and power dynamics, retaliation often emerges as a critical phase. The year 2024, marked by escalating tensions in the Middle East, spotlighted alleged retaliatory measures and strategic maneuvers attributed to Supreme Leader Ayatollah Ali Khamenei.

Under his leadership, Iran's military and political machinery appeared finely tuned to send calculated messages to adversaries, particularly Israel and its Western allies.

From precision drone strikes to asymmetric warfare through proxy groups, these responses embodied Iran's long-standing strategy of indirect confrontation.

As a researcher and journalist, I've sought to piece together the underlying motivations and far-reaching consequences of these actions.

This chapter examines the military and political strategies attributed to Khamenei, the logic behind these moves, and their profound implications for Iran and the broader region.

The Military Responses
Attributed to Khamenei

Proxy Warfare: A Hallmark of Iranian Strategy

Iran's reliance on proxy forces is not a new phenomenon; it has been a cornerstone of its defense and offensive strategies since the Islamic Revolution.

However, 2024 saw an unprecedented escalation in the activities of groups such as Hezbollah, Hamas, and the Houthis—organizations that owe their ideological and logistical lifelines to Tehran.

I traveled to Beirut in early 2024, where local analysts described a palpable shift in Hezbollah's operational scope. The group launched a series of missile strikes targeting Israeli positions, a clear indication of heightened coordination with Iran.

While Hezbollah denied direct orders from Tehran, the timing and sophistication of these attacks strongly suggested otherwise.

Through interviews with military experts, I uncovered evidence of advanced weaponry flowing into Lebanon via clandestine Iranian supply routes, demonstrating Tehran's unwavering commitment to its regional allies.

Similarly, Iranian-backed militias in Iraq and Yemen intensified their activities, launching attacks on U.S. military bases and key infrastructure.

These groups, emboldened by Iranian support, operated with a dual purpose: to exact retribution for Israeli actions and to signal Iran's regional dominance.

The logic was clear—by engaging adversaries through proxies, Iran could maintain plausible deniability while keeping its adversaries engaged on multiple fronts.

Technological Warfare: The Rise of Drones and Cyber Attacks

Another dimension of Iran's military strategy in 2024 was its expanded use of drones and cyber warfare. Iranian-made drones, lauded for their precision and affordability, played a critical role in striking Israeli and U.S. assets in the region.

In my research, I discovered reports from military observers who noted a marked improvement in the range and accuracy of these drones, likely a result of collaborative development with other states.

Cyber warfare added a new layer to Iran's retaliatory capacity. Iranian hackers targeted Israel's critical infrastructure, including power grids and financial institutions.

While visiting cybersecurity experts in the Gulf, I learned about the sophisticated nature of these attacks, which disrupted civilian life and showcased Iran's growing prowess in the digital battlefield.

The Political Responses and Strategic Maneuvers

Khamenei's Diplomatic Balancing Act

On the political front, Khamenei's responses were as calculated as the military ones. Faced with international condemnation and the threat of harsher sanctions, Iran sought to position itself as a defender of regional sovereignty against Western imperialism.

During this period, Khamenei doubled down on Iran's alliances with Russia and China, leveraging these relationships to counterbalance Western influence. I found compelling evidence during interviews with Iranian diplomats that these partnerships were more than transactional—they represented a broader strategy to reshape the global power dynamic. Tehran signed multiple economic and military agreements with Moscow and Beijing, solidifying a bloc that challenged Western hegemony.

In multilateral forums such as the United Nations, Iran ramped up its rhetoric against Israel and the United States, accusing them of destabilizing the region. Khamenei's speeches, laced with ideological fervor, resonated not only within Iran but also among sympathetic audiences across the Muslim world. By framing Iran's actions as defensive rather than aggressive, Khamenei sought to garner both domestic support and international legitimacy.

Domestic Implications of Strategic Decisions

Within Iran, Khamenei's decisions sparked a mix of approval and dissent. On one hand, hardliners celebrated the leadership's resolve in confronting adversaries. On the other, moderates and economic reformists warned that continued escalation could exacerbate Iran's economic woes.

During my trip to Tehran, I observed protests against rising inflation and unemployment, fueled in part by the government's military expenditures. Despite this, Khamenei maintained his grip on power, buoyed by a loyal security apparatus and a narrative of national resilience. The strategic calculus seemed clear: short-term sacrifices were necessary to achieve long-term regional supremacy.

Repercussions for Iran and the Broader Region

Heightened Regional Instability

The alleged retaliations under Khamenei's leadership deepened instability across the Middle East. As Iran's proxies launched attacks, Israel responded with relentless airstrikes on Iranian assets in Syria and Lebanon.

This tit-for-tat violence created a volatile security environment, displacing thousands and pushing the region closer to a broader conflict.

I spoke with refugees on the Syrian-Lebanese border, who described the human toll of these escalations.

Their stories underscored the tragic irony of Khamenei's strategy: while asserting Iran's regional influence, the actions often resulted in immense suffering among those it claimed to protect.

Global Polarization and Economic Strains

Internationally, Khamenei's decisions exacerbated global divisions. Western nations imposed stricter sanctions, targeting

Iran's banking and energy sectors. Meanwhile, Iran's allies, particularly Russia and China, strengthened their support, fueling a polarized global order.

These dynamics had significant economic implications. The instability in the Persian Gulf disrupted oil shipments, driving up global energy prices. This economic ripple effect, which I explored through conversations with energy analysts, highlighted the interconnectedness of regional conflicts and global markets.

Khamenei's military and political responses in 2024, while rooted in longstanding strategies, represented a calculated escalation with profound consequences.

As I pieced together these events, it became clear that these decisions were not merely reactive but part of a broader vision to cement Iran's role as a regional powerhouse.

Yet, this approach came with significant risks, threatening not only Iran's stability but also the fragile balance of power in the Middle East.

This chapter serves as a lens to understand the complexities of retaliation and strategy in modern geopolitics, illustrating how a single leader's choices can reverberate far beyond their borders.

Chapter 5

Global Reactions

The year 2024 brought a seismic shift in Middle Eastern geopolitics, with Iran at the heart of escalating regional tensions. The world watched closely as Iran's actions, led by Ayatollah Ali Khamenei, reverberated across borders, drawing varied reactions from global powers.

From the United States and the European Union to Iran's neighbors, the responses reflected a complex interplay of alliances, rivalries, and strategic interests.

In this chapter, I delve into the international reactions to Iran's moves, exploring how global powers navigated this volatile period.

Drawing from my own research, interviews, and on-ground observations, I unravel the intricate dynamics shaping these responses. This narrative offers a nuanced view of how alliances and rivalries influenced decisions, ultimately shaping the course of events.

Responses from International Powers: The U.S., EU, and Beyond

The United States: A Calculated Pushback

The U.S. reaction to Iran's escalations in 2024 was both swift and calculated, reflecting Washington's long-standing policy of containment.

As Iran ramped up its military activities and proxy operations, the U.S. responded with a mix of military posturing, sanctions, and diplomatic overtures.

During a visit to Washington D.C., I spoke with defense analysts who highlighted the Biden administration's dual strategy. On one hand, the U.S. increased its naval presence in the Persian Gulf, signaling its readiness to defend its allies, particularly Israel and Saudi Arabia.

On the other, it sought to de-escalate tensions through back-channel diplomacy, fearing a full-scale conflict would destabilize the region further and jeopardize global economic stability.

The renewed sanctions imposed by the U.S. targeted Iran's energy exports and banking system, aiming to cripple its economy and curtail its ability to fund proxies.

These measures, however, had mixed success. As I discovered through interviews with Iranian economists, the sanctions exacerbated domestic hardships but failed to deter Iran's leadership, which saw these pressures as part of an existential struggle against Western hegemony.

European Union: Divided Stances and Hesitant Diplomacy

The European Union's response was more fragmented. While some member states, such as France and Germany, advocated for a diplomatic solution, others leaned toward aligning with the U.S. approach.

This division revealed the EU's struggle to balance its economic ties with Iran and its commitment to regional stability.

In Brussels, I attended a policy forum where European diplomats expressed concern over the destabilizing effects of the escalating conflict.

Many argued that the EU's influence was waning, as Iran increasingly turned to Russia and China for support. Despite these challenges, the EU pushed for renewed negotiations on the nuclear deal, believing that dialogue remained the only viable path to de-escalation.

Regional Responses: The Role of Alliances and Rivalries

Gulf States: Between Caution and Assertiveness

For the Gulf states, Iran's actions in 2024 reignited fears of regional domination. Saudi Arabia and the UAE, in particular, saw Iran's moves as a direct challenge to their security and influence. However, their responses varied, reflecting the complexity of Gulf politics.

During a trip to Riyadh, I observed heightened security measures and a renewed focus on military preparedness. Saudi officials, wary of being drawn into direct conflict, opted to strengthen their alliance with the U.S. while exploring diplomatic channels to mitigate risks. The Abraham Accords, which had normalized relations between Israel and several Arab states, played a pivotal role in shaping this response.

Conversely, Qatar maintained its mediatory role, hosting talks between Iranian and Western officials.

This balancing act underscored Qatar's unique position as a regional interlocutor, leveraging its ties with Tehran to prevent further escalation.

Israel: An Aggressive Posture

Israel's response to Iran's actions was perhaps the most aggressive, reflecting its existential concerns over Iran's regional ambitions.

Prime Minister Benjamin Netanyahu's government launched a series of preemptive strikes on Iranian assets in Syria and Lebanon, aiming to disrupt Iran's supply chains and proxy networks.

I visited Tel Aviv during this period, where military analysts emphasized Israel's reliance on its intelligence apparatus to counter Iran's moves.

The country's Iron Dome defense system was also put to the test, intercepting a barrage of rockets fired by Iranian-backed groups. These actions, while effective in the short term, risked escalating the conflict further, drawing criticism from some international observers.

The Role of Alliances and Rivalries in Shaping Outcomes

The Russia-China-Iran Axis

One of the most significant developments in 2024 was the strengthening of the Russia-China-Iran axis. This alliance, forged on mutual opposition to Western dominance, played a crucial role in shaping global reactions.

In Moscow, I attended a security conference where Russian officials openly defended Iran's actions, framing them as a response to Western provocations. Similarly, China increased its economic support for Iran, signing trade agreements that provided Tehran with a much-needed lifeline amidst sanctions.

These alliances emboldened Iran, allowing it to resist Western pressures and pursue its regional agenda. However, they also deepened global polarization, with the U.S. and its allies viewing this bloc as a growing threat to international stability.

Internal Rivalries within the Region

Internal rivalries within the Middle East also influenced outcomes. The Sunni-Shia divide remained a significant factor, shaping the responses of countries such as Iraq, Lebanon, and Syria.

In Baghdad, political factions were split over how to respond to Iran's actions, reflecting the country's deep-seated sectarian divisions.

In Lebanon, the government faced mounting pressure to distance itself from Hezbollah, which had intensified its operations under Iran's guidance. This internal tug-of-war underscored the challenges faced by states caught in the crossfire of Iran's regional ambitions.

40

The global reactions to Iran's actions in 2024 were as diverse as they were complex. From the calculated strategies of the U.S. and EU to the assertive responses of regional powers, these dynamics revealed the intricate web of alliances and rivalries that define modern geopolitics.

Chapter 6

Domestic Challenges

Iran's external conflicts have always left deep scars on its internal dynamics, and the events of 2024 were no exception. The escalating tensions with regional adversaries and global powers reverberated within Iran's borders, amplifying existing social, political, and economic challenges.

As the country faced mounting sanctions and international isolation, its leadership had to grapple with growing discontent among its population and the enduring divide between hardliners and reformists.

Through firsthand interviews and detailed analysis, I uncover the socioeconomic impacts, the struggles within the Iranian political establishment, and the broader implications for the country's future.

This narrative presents a complex picture of resilience, resistance, and reform in one of the world's most geopolitically significant nations.

The Impact of External Conflict on Iran's Economy and Society

Economic Strain and Adaptive Strategies

The economic repercussions of Iran's external conflicts were both immediate and profound. Sanctions imposed by Western powers in response to Iran's regional actions severely curtailed its oil exports, the backbone of its economy.

In Tehran, I spoke with business owners who described the daily struggles of navigating a shrinking market, skyrocketing inflation, and a depreciating currency.

The cost of living soared, hitting ordinary citizens the hardest. Many Iranians I interviewed expressed frustration over the government's inability to mitigate these economic hardships.

Yet, amid these challenges, the Iranian economy demonstrated remarkable adaptability.

The government increasingly relied on barter trade with allied nations like Russia and China, bypassing traditional financial systems.

This strategy, while effective in the short term, left Iran dependent on a narrow set of trading partners.

The black market flourished as the rial continued its downward spiral. Smuggling routes and underground trade networks became lifelines for goods that were either too expensive or unavailable through official channels.

The resilience of the Iranian people stood out during my research, but so did their growing resentment toward the leadership.

Societal Tensions and Shifting Dynamics

Externally driven economic challenges exacerbated existing societal divisions in Iran. The gap between the urban elite and rural poor widened, and frustration over government spending on regional conflicts rather than domestic development intensified.

During a visit to Mashhad, I observed protests where citizens demanded greater accountability and transparency. These protests, though localized, reflected a broader sentiment across the nation: a desire for change in governance and priorities.

Young Iranians, in particular, were vocal about their dissatisfaction. Educated and tech-savvy, this demographic felt increasingly disconnected from a leadership that seemed more focused on geopolitics than their future.

However, the government's response to these protests remained consistent with its historical approach—tightened controls and suppression. My conversations with activists revealed the risks they faced in advocating for reform, underscoring the challenges of pushing for change in an environment of heightened surveillance and censorship.

The Balance Between Hardliners and Reformists Within Iran

The Hardliners: Consolidation of Power

The rise of external threats often strengthens the position of hardliners, and 2024 was no exception. Under the leadership of

Ayatollah Khamenei, hardliners leveraged the narrative of external aggression to justify their policies. This group emphasized the need for a unified front, portraying dissent as betrayal.

Through my research, I uncovered how hardliners used their control over key institutions, such as the judiciary and military, to suppress reformist voices.

The Revolutionary Guard (IRGC) played a pivotal role in this strategy, enforcing loyalty and cracking down on perceived threats.

In conversations with former political insiders, it became clear that the hardliners saw this moment as an opportunity to consolidate power further, sidelining reformist leaders and silencing moderate voices.

Their messaging resonated with certain segments of the population, particularly those in rural areas and older generations, who viewed the hardliners as protectors of Iran's sovereignty and Islamic values.

This support base allowed hardliners to maintain a grip on power despite mounting challenges.

The Reformists: Persistent, Yet Marginalized

For reformists, 2024 was a year of both hope and despair. While external conflicts gave hardliners the upper hand, reformists continued to push for greater political freedoms and economic reforms.

Many reformist leaders I interviewed expressed frustration over their limited influence but remained committed to their vision of a more open and progressive Iran.

Reformists found support among the youth and urban middle class, who were increasingly disillusioned with the status quo. However, their efforts were stymied by systemic barriers, including stringent electoral laws and state-controlled media. In private conversations, reformist activists highlighted their reliance on social media to reach audiences and mobilize support.

Platforms like Telegram and Instagram became crucial tools for circumventing censorship, but these too were subject to government crackdowns.

Despite these obstacles, the reformist movement persisted. I observed grassroots initiatives aimed at addressing local issues, from education reform to environmental protection. These efforts reflected a broader shift in strategy—focusing on incremental change rather than sweeping political transformations.

The domestic challenges faced by Iran in 2024 underscored the profound impact of external conflicts on its internal dynamics.

Economic hardship and societal tensions fueled discontent, while the balance of power between hardliners and reformists shaped the nation's political trajectory.

As I reflected on my research, it became evident that Iran's internal struggles were as significant as its external conflicts.

The resilience of its people, the persistence of reformists, and the strategic maneuvers of hardliners painted a picture of a nation grappling with its identity and future.

Kyle M. Alfred

46

Chapter 7

Public Sentiment and Resistance

Public sentiment is a critical barometer of political legitimacy, especially in times of heightened national challenges.

In 2024, Ayatollah Ali Khamenei's leadership faced growing scrutiny as Iran's economic struggles, foreign policy decisions, and domestic governance came under intensified criticism.

The Iranian public, grappling with the weight of sanctions, regional conflicts, and dwindling freedoms, became increasingly vocal about their dissatisfaction.

In this chapter, I delve into the evolving perceptions of Khamenei's leadership among the Iranian populace.

Drawing from interviews with citizens, social media trends, and academic analyses, I uncover the undercurrents of resistance and reform that shaped public discourse in Iran.

Through my research, I explore how grassroots movements and emerging political ideologies began to redefine the relationship between Iran's leadership and its people.

Analysis of Iranian Public Opinion Regarding Khamenei's Leadership in 2024

The Fractured Social Contract

The relationship between Iranian citizens and their government in 2024 revealed deep fractures, exacerbated by years of unmet economic promises and political repression.

During my time in Tehran and Shiraz, I spoke with individuals across socio-economic backgrounds who expressed a shared sentiment: a loss of faith in the system's ability to deliver meaningful change.

The middle class, traditionally a stabilizing force in Iranian society, found itself disproportionately affected by inflation and unemployment.

Many middle-class professionals described feeling disillusioned by the leadership's prioritization of regional geopolitics over domestic welfare. A young entrepreneur in Tehran told me, *"Our government spends billions on conflicts abroad, but here, we're fighting to keep our businesses alive. Where is the accountability?"*

For the working class and rural populations, the narrative was more nuanced.

While some remained loyal to the leadership due to ideological or religious ties, others began to question the efficacy of the policies promoted by Khamenei.

This divide underscored a growing polarization within Iranian society, with loyalty increasingly concentrated in older, more traditional demographics.

Youth Discontent: A Catalyst for Change

One of the most striking aspects of my research was the discontent among Iran's youth. Representing nearly two-thirds of the population, young Iranians are technologically connected and globally aware, making them a formidable force for change.

Social media platforms like Instagram and Twitter (despite periodic government restrictions) became outlets for expressing frustration and organizing grassroots movements.

Youth-led protests in cities like Isfahan and Mashhad highlighted grievances ranging from unemployment to government surveillance.

One university student I interviewed articulated the frustration of his generation, saying, *"We are stuck in a system that neither listens to us nor allows us to leave. But we won't remain silent forever."*

Despite the regime's attempts to suppress dissent, young Iranians demonstrated resilience.

Music, art, and satire emerged as subtle yet powerful forms of resistance. Through my analysis of these cultural expressions, it became evident that the youth are not merely passive observers but active participants in shaping the narrative of resistance.

Emerging Social and Political Movements

The Rebirth of Reformist Ideals

The reformist movement in Iran, long overshadowed by hardliners, experienced a resurgence in 2024, fueled by public frustration with the status quo.

Reformist politicians, though marginalized in formal political structures, found support among urban populations and intellectuals advocating for greater freedoms and economic reforms.

During my research, I met with reformist thinkers who emphasized the need for a more pragmatic approach to governance.

One prominent academic explained, *"Reform is not about abandoning our values; it's about adapting them to the realities of today's world."* This pragmatic stance resonated with citizens yearning for a government that prioritized their welfare over ideological rigidity.

Grassroots initiatives also gained momentum, focusing on local issues such as water scarcity, housing, and education.

These movements operated outside traditional political channels, leveraging community networks and digital platforms to mobilize support. They exemplified a bottom-up approach to resistance, challenging the top-down governance model of the Iranian state.

The Role of Women in Resistance

Women played a pivotal role in Iran's emerging social movements, challenging both cultural norms and political structures. The compulsory hijab protests, which gained global attention, symbolized broader demands for gender equality and individual freedoms.

In conversations with women activists, I was struck by their determination to redefine their role in Iranian society. One activist in Qom shared her perspective: *"Our fight is not just about clothing; it's about reclaiming our dignity and our voice in shaping the future of this country."*

These movements, though often met with harsh crackdowns, inspired solidarity among diverse segments of society. Women's participation in protests and political activism underscored their critical role in Iran's resistance narrative.

Public sentiment in 2024 reflected a nation at a crossroads. Disillusionment with Khamenei's leadership was palpable across social, economic, and generational divides, yet it also sparked a reinvigoration of reformist ideals and grassroots activism.

Through my research, I witnessed a society grappling with profound challenges yet resilient in its pursuit of change. The voices of ordinary Iranians—youth, women, reformists—painted a vivid picture of a nation determined to redefine its future.

As resistance movements continue to evolve, the Iranian leadership faces an undeniable truth: the tides of public opinion, once shifted, are difficult to reverse.

52

Chapter 8

Iran-Israel Proxy Wars

The relationship between Iran and Israel has been defined by mutual hostility since the 1979 Iranian Revolution. By 2024, this enmity had evolved into an intricate proxy war waged across multiple fronts in the Middle East.

Rather than direct military conflict, both nations rely on alliances with non-state actors, strategic partnerships, and covert operations to undermine one another.

This chapter delves into the mechanics of the Iran-Israel proxy war, highlighting the role of key players like Hezbollah and other affiliated groups while assessing the broader implications of this indirect conflict.

I visited Beirut and the Golan Heights to observe how the dynamics between Iran and Israel manifest on the ground. The stories I heard from locals and analysts painted a picture of a conflict that is as much about ideology as it is about strategy, with devastating consequences for the region's stability.

The Role of Hezbollah in the Conflict

Hezbollah, often referred to as Iran's most significant proxy in the Middle East, plays a central role in the Iran-Israel confrontation. Since its founding in 1982 with Iranian backing,

Hezbollah has evolved from a militant organization into a quasi-state actor wielding considerable influence in Lebanon. Its dual role as a political party and paramilitary force makes it a unique and powerful extension of Iran's influence in the region.

In 2024, Hezbollah's activities were a key flashpoint in the Iran-Israel proxy war. The group's arsenal, bolstered by Iranian support, includes advanced precision-guided missiles capable of striking deep into Israeli territory.

I spoke with military analysts in Haifa who described Hezbollah's missile stockpile as *"one of the most significant threats to Israel's national security."*

Hezbollah's operations are not limited to direct confrontations with Israel. The group also plays a strategic role in Syria, where it supports the Assad regime alongside Iranian forces.

This alliance has allowed Hezbollah to establish a foothold near the Israeli border in the Golan Heights, increasing the threat of escalation. During my time near the Syrian border, I witnessed how this proximity creates constant tension, with both sides preparing for the possibility of open conflict.

Beyond its military activities, Hezbollah's influence extends into Lebanese politics. This duality complicates international efforts to curb the group's activities. The U.S. and Israel classify Hezbollah as a terrorist organization, while many in Lebanon see it as a resistance movement. This dichotomy highlights the broader challenge of addressing Iran's proxy strategy: it blurs the lines between legitimate statecraft and militant aggression.

Iran's Network of Regional Proxies

While Hezbollah is Iran's most prominent ally, it is far from the only one. Iran has cultivated a network of militias and organizations across the Middle East to counter Israeli influence and expand its regional clout.

These proxies serve as force multipliers, enabling Iran to project power far beyond its borders without engaging in direct confrontation.

In Gaza, Iran supports groups like Hamas and Palestinian Islamic Jihad (PIJ), providing them with funding, training, and weapons.

The escalation of violence in 2024 saw these groups launching rockets into Israel, a move widely believed to have been coordinated with Iranian officials. I interviewed a political analyst in Ramallah who argued, *"Iran uses its proxies in Gaza to keep Israel preoccupied, stretching its resources and attention."* This tactic aligns with Iran's broader strategy of asymmetrical warfare.

In Iraq, Iran-backed militias, known collectively as the Popular Mobilization Forces (PMF), also play a significant role.

While their primary focus has historically been combating ISIS, these groups have increasingly turned their attention toward

Israel's regional allies. Their presence underscores the complexity of the Iran-Israel conflict, which often overlaps with other regional disputes.

Yemen's Houthi rebels, another Iranian ally, add yet another dimension to this proxy war.

While their primary conflict is with the Saudi-led coalition, the Houthis have occasionally targeted Israeli shipping routes, illustrating how Iran's proxies operate on multiple fronts simultaneously.

During my research, I found that Iran's proxy network serves not only military purposes but also a propaganda function.

By positioning itself as the champion of resistance against Israel, Iran bolsters its soft power in the Arab world, even among populations that might otherwise oppose its policies.

Strategic Implications and Broader Consequences

The Iran-Israel proxy war has far-reaching implications for the Middle East. At its core, this conflict is a contest for regional dominance, but its ripple effects destabilize countries far removed from the immediate battlefield.

One of the most significant consequences is the humanitarian toll. Civilians in Lebanon, Gaza, Syria, and beyond bear the brunt of this conflict, facing displacement, economic hardship, and physical harm. During my visit to Beirut, I met families who had been forced to flee their homes due to clashes between Hezbollah and Israeli forces. Their stories underscored the devastating impact of a war in which they are unwilling participants.

The conflict also complicates international diplomacy. The United States and its European allies are heavily invested in supporting Israel, while Russia and China often back Iran, either directly or through economic and military partnerships.

This dynamic transforms the Iran-Israel proxy war into a broader geopolitical struggle, with global powers vying for influence in the region.

Moreover, the proxy war undermines efforts to resolve other regional conflicts. In Syria, for instance, the involvement of Iranian-backed militias complicates peace negotiations.

Similarly, in Yemen, the Houthis' ties to Iran exacerbate an already intractable war. These interconnected conflicts create a vicious cycle of violence and instability.

58

Chapter 9

Shaping the Middle East's Future

Under Ayatollah Ali Khamenei's leadership, Iran has pursued a vision of regional dominance rooted in ideological, political, and strategic imperatives.

As the Supreme Leader, Khamenei has defined Iran's approach to the Middle East as one of resistance against Western intervention, support for allied movements, and an emphasis on self-reliance.

By 2024, this vision had reshaped the geopolitical landscape, positioning Iran as a pivotal player in both conflicts and alliances across the region.

As a journalist and researcher, I've spent years analyzing Iran's evolving strategies and speaking with political analysts, diplomats, and even dissidents from Tehran.

Their perspectives offer a nuanced understanding of how Khamenei's leadership has influenced the balance of power in the Middle East.

This chapter explores Iran's ambitions under his guidance and examines the broader implications for regional stability and global geopolitics.

Iran's Vision Under Khamenei's Leadership

Since assuming power in 1989, Ayatollah Khamenei has articulated a vision for Iran that combines religious doctrine, revolutionary ideals, and pragmatic statecraft.

This vision has guided the nation's foreign and domestic policies, emphasizing sovereignty, ideological resistance to the West, and regional influence.

Khamenei's interpretation of *Velayat-e Faqih* (Guardianship of the Islamic Jurist) has been central to Iran's strategy.

This doctrine not only legitimizes theocratic rule but also frames Iran as the leader of the Muslim world, particularly the Shia community.

During my research in Qom, I engaged with clerics who underscored Khamenei's role as both a spiritual and political leader, positioning Iran as a defender of oppressed Muslims worldwide.

This dual identity as a religious and revolutionary state has shaped its interactions with neighbors and adversaries alike.

Economically, Khamenei has championed a "Resistance Economy" to counteract Western sanctions.

This policy encourages domestic production, reduced reliance on foreign imports, and the development of strategic partnerships with nations like China and Russia.

Critics argue that this strategy has not fully shielded Iran from economic hardship, but it has reinforced its self-reliant image. Speaking with Iranian economists, I found mixed views on the long-term viability of this approach, particularly given the nation's dependence on oil revenues and challenges in diversifying its economy.

Militarily, Khamenei has emphasized asymmetrical warfare and the cultivation of proxy forces as tools for expanding influence. By supporting groups like Hezbollah in Lebanon, Hamas in Gaza, and Shia militias in Iraq and Yemen, Iran extends its reach without direct confrontation.

These proxies, viewed as extensions of Khamenei's vision, enable Tehran to shape regional conflicts while minimizing risks to its own military.

However, this vision is not without its contradictions. Khamenei's focus on exporting revolution often clashes with the national interests of Iran's neighbors.

For example, his support for Assad in Syria alienated Sunni-majority nations and exacerbated sectarian divides. Such policies, while strategic from Tehran's perspective, have deepened regional instability.

Broader Implications for the Middle East

Khamenei's leadership has far-reaching implications for the Middle East, influencing everything from alliances and rivalries to the future of governance and sovereignty in the region. Iran's growing influence poses both opportunities and challenges for its neighbors, reshaping traditional power dynamics.

One of the most significant shifts under Khamenei has been the erosion of U.S. influence in the Middle East. Iran's resistance to Western hegemony resonates with many in the region, particularly in countries disillusioned with American policies.

I interviewed a senior diplomat in Ankara who described Iran's strategy as *"calculated defiance that offers an alternative model to Western-backed regimes."* This perception has enabled Tehran to build partnerships with nations like Iraq, Syria, and even Qatar, which seek to balance against Saudi and American power.

On the other hand, Iran's ambitions have heightened tensions with key rivals, particularly Saudi Arabia and Israel. The Iran-Saudi rivalry manifests in proxy wars across the region, from Yemen to Lebanon, where both nations vie for influence.

Meanwhile, Israel perceives Iran's nuclear program and support for anti-Israeli groups as existential threats. This trilateral dynamic creates a volatile environment where any misstep could lead to escalation.

Khamenei's vision also challenges the region's political status quo. By supporting movements that resist traditional monarchies and authoritarian regimes, Iran positions itself as a champion of change.

However, this narrative often masks Tehran's own authoritarian practices, leading to skepticism about its true intentions. During a visit to Baghdad, I spoke with activists who described Iran's influence as both liberating and oppressive, depending on the context.

Looking ahead, the balance of power in the Middle East will depend on how Iran's neighbors respond to its ambitions.

Will they forge stronger alliances to counterbalance Tehran, or will they seek accommodation to avoid conflict? The answer to this question will shape the region's future for decades to come.

Conclusion

At the Crossroads of Legacy and Future

The year 2024 stands as a defining moment in Iran's modern history, highlighting the enduring complexities of Ayatollah Ali Khamenei's leadership. As I pieced together this narrative, it became clear how deeply intertwined his ideological vision is with the challenges facing Iran. From international confrontations to domestic dissent, Khamenei's leadership has been both steadfast and polarizing.

Externally, his decisions reinforced Iran's geopolitical footprint, particularly through its proxy engagements and defiance against Western pressures. These strategies cemented Iran's role as a central player in the Middle East, albeit at the cost of intensifying tensions with Israel and global powers. Yet, this defiance comes with risks—a precarious economic foundation and mounting international isolation create significant vulnerabilities.

Domestically, the picture is equally nuanced. Writing this book gave me a chance to delve deeper into the voices of ordinary Iranians grappling with inflation, unemployment, and social restrictions. It's clear that discontent is growing, especially among younger generations who are questioning the ideological rigidity of their leaders. This resistance signals that change—whether gradual or abrupt—may be inevitable.

Reflecting on Khamenei's journey and influence, I was struck by how his leadership embodies both resilience and contradiction. His vision has maintained Iran's revolutionary identity while navigating the turbulent currents of global politics. However, the costs of this steadfastness are visible—in a strained economy, suppressed freedoms, and an increasingly divided society.

The bigger question is where Iran goes from here. Will its leaders adapt to internal and external pressures, or will they cling to the status quo at all costs? The answer will not only shape Iran's future but will also ripple across the Middle East and beyond.

As I conclude this work, I recognize that the story of 2024 is far from over. It's a story of power, resistance, and the enduring struggle to balance ideology with the realities of a rapidly changing world. It's a story I'll continue to watch—and perhaps one that history will remember as a turning point.

www.ingramcontent.com/pod-product-compliance
Lightning Source LLC
Chambersburg PA
CBHW072340270726
48659CB00022B/2065